BRITAIN'S
BEST-LOVED
Comic Poems

~ Acknowledgements ~

The publishers would like to acknowledge the following
for permission to reproduce copyright material.

14. 'Curl Up and Diet' from *Candy is Dandy* by Ogden
    Nash, published by Andre Deutsch Ltd (1983).
24. 'On the Ning Nang Nong' from *Silly Verse for Kids* by Spike
    Milligan, published by Puffin Books (1968). Reprinted by
    permission of Spike Milligan Productions Ltd.
37. 'The Frog' from *Complete Verse* by Hilaire Belloc,
    published by Random House UK Ltd. Reprinted by
    permission of PFD on behalf of: *The Estate of Hilaire
    Belloc*. © Estate of Hilaire Belloc.
41. 'Bloody Men' from *Serious Concerns* by Wendy Cope.
    Reprinted by permission of Faber and Faber Ltd.
42. 'Nobody loses all the time' is reprinted from *Complete
    Poems 1904–1962* by E.E. Cummings, edited by George
    J. Firmage, by permission of W.W. Norton & Company.
    Copyright © 1991 by the Trustees for the E.E. Cummings
    Trust and George James Firmage.
49. 'Talking Turkeys!!' from *Talking Turkeys* by Benjamin
    Zephaniah (Viking, 1994). © Benjamin Zephaniah, 1994.
    Reproduced by permission of Penguin Books.

The publishers have made every effort to trace copyright
holders of material reproduced within this compilation.
If, however, they have inadvertently made any error they
would be grateful for notification.

BRITAIN'S
BEST-LOVED
Comic Poems

Produced by BBC Books, BBC Worldwide Ltd
Woodlands, 80 Wood Lane
London W12 0TT

First published in 2004
This edition published for
Marks & Spencer plc, 2004
P O Box 3339, Chester CH99 9QS
www.marksandspencer.com
Compilation © BBC Books, BBC Worldwide Ltd 2004
Poems © individual copyright holders

The publishers would like to thank the Mary Evans
Picture Library for permission to reproduce the
images that appear in this book.

ISBN 0 563 52224 0

Commissioning editors: Nicky Ross and Emma Shackleton
Project editors: Warren Albers and Anthea Bull
Designer: Ann Burnham

Set in Cantoria MT and Plantin
Printed and bound in Italy by L.E.G.O. spa

Contents

contents

Introduction

A chuckle is good, a giggle better, but nothing beats a hearty belly-laugh brought on by a good punchline, some sparkling wit, wry humour, or just plain, outlandish nonsense.

This little collection of poems has been specially put together to tickle your funny-bone. From Thomas Moore's pithy 'On taking a wife' to the limericks of Edward Lear and Benjamin Zephaniah's 'Talking turkeys!!', this mini-treasury of fun is packed with verse that is certain to bring a smile to your face.

On Mary Ann

Mary Ann has gone to rest,
Safe at last on Abraham's breast,
Which may be nuts for Mary Ann,
But is certainly rough on Abraham.

ANON

Limericks

(i)

There was an Old Man in a boat,
Who said, 'I'm afloat! I'm afloat!'
    When they said, 'No! you ain't!'
        he was ready to faint,
That unhappy Old Man in a boat.

(ii)

There was a young person whose history,
Was always considered a mystery;
    She sate in a ditch,
        although no one knew which,
And composed a small treatise on history.

(iii)

There was an Old Man of Toulouse
Who purchased a new pair of shoes;
When they asked, 'Are they pleasant?'
– He said, 'Not at present!'
That turbid old man of Toulouse.

(iv)

There was a Young Lady of Portugal,
Whose ideas were excessively nautical:
She climbed up a tree,
to examine the sea,
But declared she would never leave Portugal.

limericks

ACME
WATFORD

(v)

There was an Old Man with a beard,

Who said, 'It is just as I feared! –

    Two Owls and a Hen,

      four Larks and a Wren,

Have all built their nests in my beard!'

(vi)

There was an Old Man of Hong Kong,

Who never did anything wrong;

    He lay on his back,

      with his head in a sack,

That innocuous Old Man of Hong Kong.

EDWARD LEAR 1812–88

Curl up and diet

Some ladies smoke too much and some ladies
    drink too much and some ladies pray too much,
But all ladies think that they weigh too much.
They may be as slender as a sylph or a dryad,
But just let them get on the scales and they
    embark on a doleful jeremiad:
No matter how low the figure the needle
    happens to touch,
They always claim it is at least five pounds
    too much;

To the world she may appear slinky and feline,
But she inspects herself in the mirror and cries,
    Oh, I look like a sea lion.
Yes, she tells you she is growing into the shape of
    a sea cow or manatee,
And if you say No, my dear, she says you are just
    lying to make her feel better, and if you say
    Yes, my dear, you injure her vanity.
Once upon a time there was a girl more beautiful
    and witty and charming than tongue can tell,

curl up and diet

And she is now a dangerous raving maniac in
    a padded cell,
And the first indication her friends and relatives
    had that she was mentally overwrought
Was one day when she said, I weigh a hundred
    and twenty-seven, which is exactly what I
    ought.
Oh, often I am haunted
By the thought that somebody might someday
    discover a diet that would let ladies reduce
    just as much as they wanted,
Because I wonder if there is a woman in the
    world strong-minded enough to shed ten
    pounds or twenty,

And say There now, that's plenty;

And I fear me one ten-pound loss would only
arouse the craving for another,

So it wouldn't do any good for ladies to get their
ambition and look like somebody's fourteen-
year-old brother,

Because, having accomplished this with ease,

They would next want to look like somebody's
fourteen-year-old brother in the final stages
of some obscure disease,

And the more success you have the more you
want to get of it,
So then their goal would be to look like somebody's
fourteen-year-old brother's ghost, or rather not
the ghost itself, which is fairly solid, but a
silhouette of it,
So I think it is very nice for ladies to be lithe and
lissome.
But not so much so that you cut yourself if you
happen to embrace or kissome.

OGDEN NASH 1902–71

On a tired housewife

Here lies a poor woman who was always tired,
She lived in a house where help wasn't hired:
Her last words on earth were: 'Dear friends,
    I am going
To where there's no cooking, or washing, or sewing,
For everything there is exact to my wishes,
For where they don't eat there's no washing of dishes.
I'll be where loud anthems will always be ringing,
But having no voice I'll be quit of the singing.
Don't mourn for me now, don't mourn for me never,
I am going to do nothing for ever and ever.'

ANON

Recipe for a salad

To make this condiment, your poet begs
The pounded yellow of two hard-boiled eggs;
Two boiled potatoes, passed through kitchen-sieve,
Smoothness and softness to the salad give;
Let onion atoms lurk within the bowl,
And, half-suspected, animate the whole.
Of mordant mustard add a single spoon,
Distrust the condiment that bites so soon;
But deem it not, thou man of herbs, a fault,
To add a double quantity of salt.

And, lastly, o'er the flavored compound toss
A magic soup-spoon of anchovy sauce.
Oh, green and glorious! Oh, herbaceous treat!
'T would tempt the dying anchorite to eat;
Back to the world he'd turn his fleeting soul,
And plunge his fingers in the salad bowl!
Serenely full, the epicure would say,
Fate can not harm me, I have dined to-day!

SYDNEY SMITH 1771–1845

On the Ning Nang Nong

On the Ning Nang Nong
Where the Cows go Bong!
And the Monkeys all say Boo!
There's a Nong Nang Ning
Where the trees go Ping!
And the tea pots Jibber Jabber Joo.
On the Nong Ning Nang
All the mice go Clang!
And you just can't catch 'em when they do!

So it's Ning Nang Nong!
Cows go Bong!
Nong Nang Ning!
Trees go Ping!
Nong Ning Nang!
The mice go Clang!
What a noisy place to belong,
Is the Ning Nang Ning Nang Nong!!

SPIKE MILLIGAN 1918–2002

Song

Go, and catch a falling star,
    Get with child a mandrake root,
Tell me, where all past years are,
    Or who cleft the Devil's foot,
Teach me to hear mermaids singing,
    Or to keep off envy's stinging,
        And find
        What wind
Serves to advance an honest mind.

If thou be'est born to strange sights,
    Things invisible to see,
Ride ten thousand days and nights,
    Till age snow white hairs on thee,
Thou, when thou return'st, wilt tell me
All strange wonders that befell thee,
        And swear
        No where
Lives a woman true, and fair.

If thou find'st one, let me know,
    Such a pilgrimage were sweet,
Yet do not, I would not go,
    Though at next door we might meet,
Though she were true, when you met her,
And last, till you write your letter,
      Yet she
      Will be
False, ere I come, to two, or three.

JOHN DONNE 1572–1631

On taking a wife

'Come, come,' said Tom's father, 'at your time of life,
　　There's no longer excuse for thus playing the rake.
It's time you should think, boy, of taking a wife.'
　　'Why so it is, father. Whose wife shall I take?'

THOMAS MOORE 1779–1852

Father William

'You are old, Father William,' the young man said,
  'And your hair has become very white;
And yet you incessantly stand on your head –
  Do you think, at your age, it is right?'

'In my youth,' Father William replied to his son,
  'I feared it might injure the brain;
But, now that I'm perfectly sure I have none,
  Why, I do it again and again.'

father william

'You are old,' said the youth, 'as I mentioned before,
　　And have grown most uncommonly fat;
Yet you turned a back-somersault in at the door –
　　Pray, what is the reason of that?'

'In my youth,' said the sage, as he shook his grey locks,
　　'I kept all my limbs very supple
By the use of this ointment – one shilling the box –
　　Allow me to sell you a couple?'

'You are old,' said the youth, 'and your jaws are too weak
　　For anything tougher than suet;
Yet you finished the goose, with the bones and the beak –
　　Pray, how did you manage to do it?'

'In my youth,' said his father, 'I took to the law,
      And argued each case with my wife;
And the muscular strength, which it gave to my jaw,
      Has lasted the rest of my life.'

'You are old,' said the youth, 'one would hardly suppose
      That your eye was as steady as ever;
Yet you balanced an eel on the end of your nose –
      What made you so awfully clever?'

'I have answered three questions, and that is enough,'
      Said his father; 'don't give yourself airs!
Do you think I can listen all day to such stuff?
      Be off, or I'll kick you down stairs!'

LEWIS CARROLL 1832–98

The frog

Be kind and tender to the Frog,
    And do not call him names,
As 'Slimy skin', or 'Polly-wog',
    Or likewise 'Ugly James',
Or 'Gap-a-grin', or 'Toad-gone-wrong',
    Or 'Billy Bandy-knees':
The Frog is justly sensitive
    To epithets like these.
No animal will more repay
    A treatment kind and fair;
At least so lonely people say
    Who keep a frog (and, by the way,
They are extremely rare).

HILAIRE BELLOC 1870–1953

King Charles II

Here lies our mutton-eating King
　　Whose word no man relies on,
Who never said a foolish thing,
　　Nor ever did a wise one.

JOHN WILMOT, EARL OF ROCHESTER 1647–80

Epigram

*Engraved on the collar of a dog which I gave to his
Royal Highness Frederick Prince of Wales*

I am his Highness' dog at Kew
Pray tell me, sir, whose dog are you?

ALEXANDER POPE 1688–1744

Bloody men

Bloody men are like bloody buses –
You wait for about a year
And as soon as one approaches your stop
Two or three others appear.

You look at them flashing their indicators,
Offering you a ride.
You're trying to read the destinations,
You haven't much time to decide.

If you make a mistake, there is no turning back.
Jump off, and you'll stand there and gaze
While the cars and the taxis and lorries go by
And the minutes, the hours, the days.

WENDY COPE 1945–

Nobody loses
all the time

nobody loses all the time

i had an uncle named
Sol who was born a failure and
nearly everybody said he should have gone
into vaudeville perhaps because my Uncle Sol could
sing McCann He Was A Diver on Xmas Eve like
    Hell Itself which
may or may not account for the fact that my Uncle

Sol indulged in that possibly most inexcusable
of all to use a highfallootin phrase
luxuries that is or to
wit farming and be
it needlessly
added

my Uncle Sol's farm
failed because the chickens
ate the vegetables so
my Uncle Sol had a
chicken farm till the
skunks ate the chickens when

nobody loses all the time

my Uncle Sol
had a skunk farm but
the skunks caught cold and
died and so
my Uncle Sol imitated the
skunks in a subtle manner

or by drowning himself in the watertank
but somebody who'd given my Uncle Sol a Victor
Victrola and records while he lived presented to
him upon the auspicious occasion of his decease a
scrumptious not to mention splendiferous funeral with
tall boys in black gloves and flowers and everything and

nobody loses all the time

i remember we all cried like the Missouri
when my Uncle Sol's coffin lurched because
somebody pressed a button
(and down went
my Uncle
Sol

and started a worm farm)

E.E. CUMMINGS 1884–1962

Peas

I always eat peas with honey,
I've done it all my life,
They do taste kind of funny,
But it keeps them on my knife.

ANON

Talking turkeys!!

Be nice to yu turkeys dis christmas
Cos turkey jus wanna hav fun
Turkeys are cool, turkeys are wicked
An every turkey has a Mum.
Be nice to yu turkeys dis christmas,
Don't eat it, keep it alive,
It could be yu mate an not on yu plate
Say, Yo! Turkey I'm on your side.

I got lots of friends who are turkeys
An all of dem fear christmas time,
Dey wanna enjoy it, dey say humans destroyed it
An humans are out of dere mind,
Yeah, I got lots of friends who are turkeys

Dey all hav a right to a life,
Not to be caged up an genetically made up
By any farmer an his wife.

Turkeys jus wanna play reggae
Turkeys jus wanna hip-hop
Can yu imagine a nice young turkey saying,
'I cannot wait for de chop'?
Turkeys like getting presents, dey wanna watch
    christmas TV,
Turkeys hav brains an turkeys feel pain
In many ways like yu an me.

I once new a turkey called Turkey
He said 'Benji explain to me please,
Who put de turkey in christmas

An what happens to christmas trees?'
I said, 'I am not too sure turkey
But it's nothing to do wid Christ Mass
Humans get greedy an waste more dan need be
An business men mek loadsa cash.'

Be nice to yu turkey dis christmas
Invite dem indoors fe sum greens
Let dem eat cake an let dem partake
In a plate of organic grown beans,
Be nice to yu turkey dis christmas
An spare dem de cut of de knife,
Join Turkeys United an dey'll be delighted
An yu will mek new friends 'FOR LIFE'.

BENJAMIN ZEPHANIAH 1958–

All these are vile

The House of Mourning written by Mr Scott,
    A sermon at the Magdalen, a tear
    Dropped on a greasy novel, want of cheer
After a walk uphill to a friend's cot,
Tea with a maiden lady, a cursed lot
    Of worthy poems with the author near,
    A patron lord, a drunkenness from beer,
Haydon's great picture, a cold coffee pot

At midnight when the muse is ripe for labour,
　　The voice of Mr Coleridge, a French bonnet
Before you in the pit, a pipe and tabour,
A damned inseparable flute and neighbour –
　　All these are vile. But viler Wordsworth's sonnet
　　On Dover. Dover! Who *could* write upon it?

JOHN KEATS 1795–1821

Mr Scott is John Scott, first editor of the London
Magazine, *which was established in 1820. The
Magdalen refers to the Magdalen Hospital, a refuge
for reformed prostitutes. Benjamin Haydon was
famous for his historical and biblical paintings.*

Doctor Fell

I do not love thee, Doctor Fell.
The reason why, I cannot tell;
But this I know, and know full well,
I do not love thee, Doctor Fell.

TOM BROWN 1663–1704

Opportunity

When Mrs Gorm (Aunt Eloise)
Was stung to death by savage bees,
Her husband (Prebendary Gorm)
Put on his veil, and took the swarm.
He's publishing a book next May
On 'How to Make Bee-keeping Pay'.

HARRY GRAHAM 1874–1936

Wishes of an elderly man, wished at a garden party, June 1914

I wish I loved the Human Race;
I wish I loved its silly face;
I wish I loved the way it walks;
I wish I loved the way it talks;
And when I'm introduced to one
I wish I thought *What Jolly Fun!*

SIR WALTER RALEIGH 1861–1922

The pig

It was an evening in November,
As I very well remember,
I was strolling down the street in drunken pride,
But my knees were all a-flutter,
And I landed in the gutter
And a pig came up and lay down by my side.

Yes, I lay there in the gutter
Thinking thoughts I could not utter,
When a colleen passing by did softly say
'You can tell a man who boozes
By the company he chooses' –
And the pig got up and slowly walked away.

ANON

My mistress' eyes are
nothing like the sun

My mistress' eyes are nothing like the sun.
Coral is far more red than her lips' red:
If snow be white, why then her breasts are dun:
If hairs be wires, black wires grow on her head.
I have seen roses damask'd, red and white,
But no such roses see I in her cheeks:
And in some perfumes is there more delight
Than in the breath that from my mistress reeks.

my mistress' eyes are nothing like the sun

I love to hear her speak, yet well I know
That music hath a far more pleasing sound:
I grant I never saw a goddess go, –
My mistress, when she walks, treads on the ground:
    And yet, by heaven, I think my love as rare
    As any she belied with false compare.

WILLIAM SHAKESPEARE 1564–1616